W9-CKI-130

Louisiana

EXPLORE THE UNITED STATES ★ EXPLORE THE UNITED STATES ★ EXPLORE THE UNITED STATES

Julie Murray

Big Buddy BOOKS
Explore the United States

VISIT US AT
www.abdopublishing.com

Published by ABDO Publishing Company, PO Box 398166, Minneapolis, MN 55439.

Copyright © 2013 by Abdo Consulting Group, Inc. International copyrights reserved in all countries. No part of this book may be reproduced in any form without written permission from the publisher. Big Buddy Books™ is a trademark and logo of ABDO Publishing Company.

Printed in the United States of America, North Mankato, Minnesota.
042012
092012

 PRINTED ON RECYCLED PAPER

Coordinating Series Editor: Rochelle Baltzer
Editor: Sarah Tieck
Contributing Editors: Megan M. Gunderson, BreAnn Rumsch, Marcia Zappa
Graphic Design: Adam Craven
Cover Photograph: *iStockphoto*: ©iStockphoto.com/dlewis33.
Interior Photographs/Illustrations: *Alamy*: Joe Vogan (p. 30); *AP Images*: AP Photo (p. 13), Virginian-Pilot, Perry Breon (p. 23), Cal Sport Media via AP Images (p. 27), North Wind Picture Archives via AP Images (p. 13), Reed Saxon, File (p. 25), Kevin Terrell (p. 21); *Getty Images*: Danita Delimont/Gallo Images (p. 30); *Glow Images*: Phillip Gould (p. 27), Egmont Strigl (p. 27), Jeremy Woodhouse (p. 11); *iStockphoto*: ©iStockphoto.com/drbimages (p. 5), ©iStockphoto.com/sf-foodphoto (p. 26), ©iStockphoto.com/DenisTangneyJr (p. 11); *Louisiana Secretary of State* (p. 30); *Shutterstock*: Thomas Barrat (p. 26), Louis Bourgeois (p. 9), Darryl Brooks (p. 30), Ed Metz (p. 9), RIRF Stock (p. 29), robcocquyt (p. 19), VT750 (p. 17).

All population figures taken from the 2010 US census.

Library of Congress Cataloging-in-Publication Data

Murray, Julie, 1969-
 Louisiana / Julie Murray.
   p. cm. -- (Explore the United States)
 ISBN 978-1-61783-356-4
 1. Louisiana--Juvenile literature. I. Title.
 F369.3.M875 2013
 976.3--dc23
                          2012005982

LOUISIANA

Contents

ONE NATION

The United States is a **diverse** country. It has farmland, cities, coasts, and mountains. Its people come from many different backgrounds. And, its history covers more than 200 years.

Today the country includes 50 states. Louisiana is one of these states. Let's learn more about Louisiana and its story!

Did You Know?

Louisiana became a state on April 30, 1812. It was the eighteenth state to join the nation.

Louisiana is famous for its swampy areas called bayous (BEYE-oos).

Louisiana Up Close

Did You Know?

Washington DC is the US capital city. Puerto Rico is a US commonwealth. This means it is governed by its own people.

The United States has four main **regions**. Louisiana is in the South.

Louisiana shares its borders with three states. Texas is west, Arkansas is north, and Mississippi is east. The Gulf of Mexico is south.

Louisiana has a total area of 47,632 square miles (123,366 sq km). About 4.5 million people live in the state.

REGIONS OF THE UNITED STATES

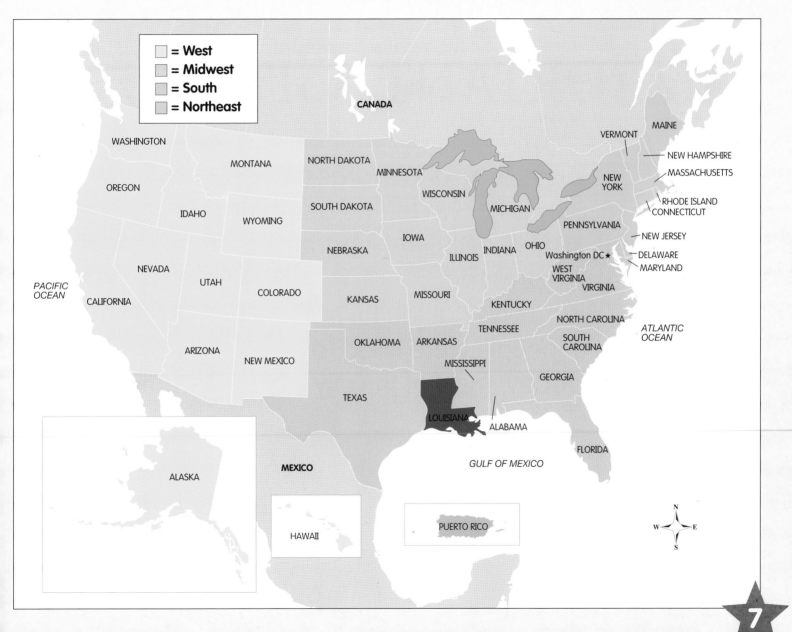

= West
= Midwest
= South
= Northeast

CANADA

PACIFIC OCEAN

WASHINGTON
OREGON
IDAHO
MONTANA
WYOMING
NEVADA
UTAH
CALIFORNIA
ARIZONA
NEW MEXICO
COLORADO

NORTH DAKOTA
SOUTH DAKOTA
NEBRASKA
KANSAS
OKLAHOMA
TEXAS

MINNESOTA
WISCONSIN
IOWA
MISSOURI
ARKANSAS
MISSISSIPPI
LOUISIANA

MICHIGAN
ILLINOIS
INDIANA
OHIO
KENTUCKY
TENNESSEE
ALABAMA

VERMONT
MAINE
NEW HAMPSHIRE
MASSACHUSETTS
NEW YORK
RHODE ISLAND
CONNECTICUT
PENNSYLVANIA
NEW JERSEY
Washington DC ★
DELAWARE
MARYLAND
WEST VIRGINIA
VIRGINIA
NORTH CAROLINA
SOUTH CAROLINA
GEORGIA
FLORIDA

ATLANTIC OCEAN

GULF OF MEXICO

MEXICO

ALASKA

HAWAII

PUERTO RICO

N
W   E
S

7

Important Cities

New Orleans is Louisiana's largest city. It has 343,829 people. This city is known for the arts, old buildings, and Mardi Gras (MAHR-dee GRAH) parades. It is also the birthplace of jazz music.

In 2005, **Hurricane** Katrina hit New Orleans. Thousands of people were killed, and much of the city was ruined. Today, most of the city has been rebuilt.

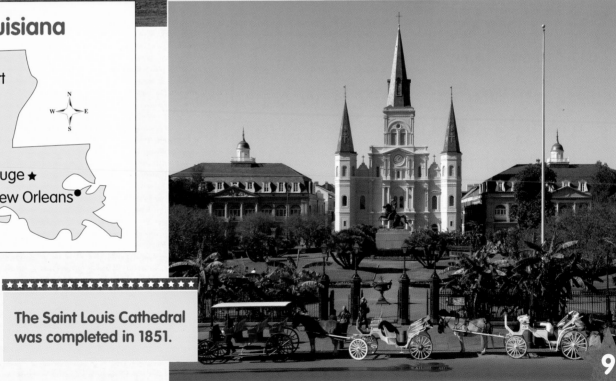

New Orleans is located at the mouth of the Mississippi River. It is a busy port.

Louisiana

● Shreveport

N
W — E
S

Baton Rouge ★
New Orleans ●

★★★★★★★★★★★★★★★★★★★★

The Saint Louis Cathedral was completed in 1851.

9

Baton Rouge is Louisiana's **capital**. It is also the state's second-largest city. Its population is 229,493. Shipping is important to this city. It is one of the main ports on the Mississippi River.

Shreveport is the state's third-largest city, with 199,311 people. It is on the Red River. The Louisiana State Fair takes place in this city every year.

Louisiana's state capitol is 34 stories! It is the tallest capitol in the United States.

Shreveport is located near where Louisiana meets Arkansas and Texas. This area is known as "Ark-La-Tex."

11

LOUISIANA IN HISTORY

Louisiana's history includes Native Americans, explorers, and settlers. Native Americans hunted and farmed in present-day Louisiana for thousands of years.

The Spanish were the first Europeans to explore the area. But, the French were the first to settle there. In 1682, the French claimed the land. In 1803, France sold it to the United States. This was called the **Louisiana Purchase**. Louisiana became a state in 1812.

Did You Know?

Louisiana's location on the Mississippi River and the Gulf of Mexico made it appealing. Many countries wanted to control it.

Hernando de Soto led a group of Spanish explorers to Louisiana in 1541. They were looking for gold.

President Thomas Jefferson arranged for the Louisiana Purchase. This almost doubled the size of the United States!

Timeline

1718

The city of New Orleans was founded.

1720

The Saint Louis Cathedral was founded in New Orleans. It is the oldest church in Louisiana.

1700s

1803

President Thomas Jefferson bought most of Louisiana as part of the **Louisiana Purchase**. This opened up new land for Americans to settle and explore.

1861

The **American Civil War** began. Louisiana fought for the Southern states.

1800s

14

1953

1869

The McIlhenny Company started selling Tabasco sauce. This spicy pepper sauce is made on Avery Island.

On June 20, African Americans in Baton Rouge started a bus **boycott**. This was one of the first events of the **civil rights movement**.

2010

An oil rig exploded in the Gulf of Mexico. Oil spilled into the water near Louisiana and washed up on beaches.

1900s

2000s

In New Orleans, boxers Andy Bowen and Jack Burke tied after fighting for 7 hours and 19 minutes. This was the longest boxing match in history.

Hurricane Katrina destroyed parts of New Orleans and the Louisiana coast.

The New Orleans Saints football team won their first Super Bowl!

2005

2010

1893

15

Across the Land

Louisiana has forests and flat, grassy land. But, this state is best known for water. There are many swamps, **marshes**, and bayous. Louisiana is also where the Mississippi River meets the Gulf of Mexico.

Many types of animals make their homes in Louisiana. These include alligators, doves, pelicans, crayfish, and shrimp.

★ **Did You Know?**

In July, Louisiana's average temperature is 82°F (28°C). In January, it is 50°F (10°C).

Bayous are very slow-moving bodies of water. Alligators live in Louisiana's bayous.

Earning a Living

Louisiana has rich farming soil. Since the 1700s, sugarcane and cotton have been important crops. Today, trees are grown for building materials.

Many people in Louisiana work in service jobs. Some have jobs helping visitors to the state. Others work in businesses such as banks and shops.

Louisiana is a leading US producer of oil and gas. Oil rigs in the Gulf of Mexico collect oil from under the ocean floor.

19

Sports Page

Many people think of sports when they think of Louisiana. That's because the state has popular football and basketball teams.

College sports also have many fans in Louisiana. The Sugar Bowl is held in New Orleans every January. This game features two top college football teams.

Did You Know?

The Super Bowl has been held in New Orleans ten times between 1970 and 2013.

The New Orleans Saints is a well-known football team. Quarterback Drew Brees led the team to many wins over the years.

HOMETOWN HEROES

Many famous people are from Louisiana. Louis Armstrong was born in New Orleans in 1901. He was a well-known jazz musician.

Armstrong first became famous in the 1920s. Some of his best-loved songs are "Hello, Dolly!" and "What a Wonderful World."

People remember Armstrong for playing the trumpet and for singing.

23

The Mannings are a famous football family that lived in New Orleans. Archie Manning was a quarterback for the New Orleans Saints for 11 seasons.

Archie's sons Eli and Peyton were born in New Orleans. Both became talented quarterbacks in the National Football League.

Archie (*center*) was a professional quarterback from 1971 to 1984. He taught Eli (*left*) and Peyton (*right*) to love playing football.

25

Tour Book

Do you want to go to Louisiana? If you visit the state, here are some places to go and things to do!

 ## See

Check out the famous French Quarter in New Orleans. This area is known for its old buildings of French and Spanish style. People celebrate Mardi Gras there every February or March.

 ## Taste

Try some Creole food. This type of food is known for being spicy. It often includes seafood, peppers, and rice. Gumbo soup (*right*) is a famous Creole dish.

 ## Remember

Visit a plantation, such as the Nottoway Plantation in White Castle. Plantations were large farms in the 1800s.

 ## Cheer

Tulane University has popular sports teams. Catch a Green Wave football game!

 ## Listen

Take in some Cajun music. Cajun bands often include accordions, fiddles, and triangles.

A GREAT STATE

The story of Louisiana is important to the United States. The people and places that make up this state offer something special to the country. Together with all the states, Louisiana helps make the United States great.

Lake Pontchartrain is one of the largest saltwater lakes in the United States.

Index